HAUS CURIOSITIES

The European Identity

ABOUT THE AUTHOR

Stephen Green was an international banker and Minister for Trade and Investment between 2011–13. He chairs the Natural History Museum, is an ordained priest of the Church of England and sits as a Conservative peer in the House of Lords. He is the author of *Reluctant Meister: How Germany's Past is Shaping its European Future*.

Stephen Green

THE EUROPEAN IDENTITY

Historical and Cultural Realities We Cannot Deny

HAUS
CURIOSITIES

First published by Haus Publishing in 2015
70 Cadogan Place
London SW1X 9AH
www.hauspublishing.com

A CIP catalogue record for this book is
available from the British Library

Print ISBN: 978-1-910376-17-1
Ebook ISBN: 978-1-910376-29-4

Typeset in Garamond by MacGuru Ltd
info@macguru.org.uk

Printed in Spain

Contents

What does it mean to be European?

Europe is the western corner of the Eurasian land mass. It has natural frontiers to the north, south and west, but not to the east. It is easiest to think of its eastern borders as being broadly those of the present-day European Union.

Are those borders permanent? Not necessarily. But Russia has a very different identity; occasionally down the centuries it has sought to convince itself and others that its outlook is essentially European, but at its heart it is the land of the steppes and forests. It has a geopolitical centre of gravity which is well to the east of Europe, and a culture moulded to this day by the Orthodox heritage which marks it out so distinctly.

And Turkey? Even in the days of old Byzantium, relations with Catholic Europe were always fractious and sometimes violent. Then came the Ottoman centuries when Turkish military expansion was the constant nightmare of Europe. Now Europe is thoroughly secularised, and Atatürk, the founder of modern Turkey, sought the same for his country. Yet recent years have shown that Turkey's secularism is much less deeply rooted. Turkey may eventually join the European Union, but the cultural challenge looks intractable to many on both sides.

So Europe effectively includes the 28 current member states of the European Union and a few other potential member states in south-east Europe, plus Norway,

Switzerland, Iceland – and a number of small entities such as Liechtenstein, Monaco and the Channel Islands, all of which are vestiges of earlier, premodern forms of sovereignty.

We need to ask ourselves whether this Europe has any real identity. For although the world of the 21st century is ever more global and interconnected, the importance of geopolitics has in no way declined. There are some old and some new great powers on the world stage. There are new actors, new cultural challenges and new sources of instability. Directly or indirectly, Europe will be impacted and profoundly challenged. How the Europeans respond will depend on what they have in common. What if anything – amidst all the kaleidoscopic variety – do we Europeans think we share? What is it to be a European in the modern age? Does it have any significance – geopolitically, commercially or culturally? What future does it have?

These are questions for all of Europe, but especially for the three leading states of the EU, for each of which they are unsettling in a unique way. For France – used to seeing itself as the moral and political leader of the European project – its whole self-understanding is in play, as the centre of gravity shifts towards a reluctant Berlin. Meanwhile, Britain has for centuries regarded the continent mostly as a threat or a distraction; but it is learning that its own identity is far more fragile than it ever realised. And for Germany, which – because of its deep history – is more truly comfortable with a multi-layered identity than either of the other two, the 20th century still casts a shadow; the role of leadership which has been thrust upon it by the facts of geography and economics still does not come at all easily.

Few people have ever thought of themselves primarily as Europeans. In the four centuries up to 1914, when Europe was the dynamic centre of the world and when Europeans fanned out over the globe to trade and conquer, they defined themselves by their religion, by their language and by their nationality (which they saw increasingly in racial – and indeed Darwinian – terms). After 1945, in the wake of the moral and physical disasters of what was in effect a second Thirty Years War at the heart of Europe, there was a new determination to achieve a robust and enduring peace. This was the vision of a small European elite, but they were responding to a widespread sense of exhaustion and disgust (which it takes a leap of imagination these days to fully comprehend). It was given effect in the embryonic structures that eventually evolved into the European Union, and blessed – initially from the sidelines – by a Britain which only belatedly, and never wholeheartedly, joined up.

Yet none of this, not even in the early visionary years, represented the emergence of a new and widely recognised European identity. In fact, there is no political appetite – in any member state, and certainly not in any of the big three – to strengthen a European sense of identity by giving any institution or individual role a clear leadership mandate at the European level. This reluctance is not born just from lingering nationalism or from theoretical concerns about the democratic legitimacy of any such mandate. It reflects something much deeper: an insistent question about what that identity is and how it should be projected.

In the last 70 years, the most pressing objective has been achieved: not only has Europe been at peace with itself, but war between the member states has become virtually unthinkable. But the sense of a European identity, though it has grown, remains weak. It is still the case (as evidenced by the official Eurobarometer surveys[1]) that majorities in every country think of themselves not primarily as Europeans but in national terms (and in the case of Britain fewer than half see their identity in European terms at all). Recent years have seen a growth in the percentage of people who see themselves as national but also European, and a decline in the percentage who see themselves as national only: but for all other than a very small minority the European identity is secondary rather than primary.

When people are asked what are the important ingredients in the European identity, half of those who are citizens of eurozone countries cite the euro. Only half as many cite history and culture. Not surprisingly, fewer than a quarter of those from non-eurozone members cite the euro, although they are about equally likely to cite history and culture. Furthermore, the trend data show that culture is on the wane as an element in people's understanding of identity: there is evidence that sport is becoming a more important factor – and it is unclear what effect this has on people's sense of a European identity.

Indeed, the case for Europe is almost never argued in terms of identity. In Britain, even the pro-Europeans argue not on the basis of common values and cultural identity, but on the basis of commerce – from the benefits of the single market and the advantage of critical mass in international trade negotiations. In France and Germany, and in the eurozone more generally, policy debate for the last few years has focussed

– for understandable reasons – largely on a near-term macro-economic imperative of stabilisation and structural reform. The urgent task has been to integrate monetary policy and coordinate fiscal policy – not in order to strengthen any European identity, but to deal with the problems of over-indebted weaker members of the eurozone (above all, Greece) and to get growth going again. The Treaty of Lisbon sets out the member states' resolve to 'continue the process of creating an ever closer union among the peoples of Europe'. But apart from rare voices like that of the influential German philosopher Jürgen Habermas (of whom more below), there are few – and no politicians of any significance anywhere – who see the creation and nurturing of a new European identity as a primary challenge, or even as having much relevance, for modern Europeans.

A whole generation has grown up since the fall of the Berlin wall – an event which led to the creation, for the first time ever, not only of a new, unified and peaceful Germany but also of a new European Union embracing almost all of the continent. It is a generation for whom borders are not restrictions, either physical or psychological – and on whose shoulders the burden of the painful past sits ever more lightly. And yet there is more existential angst than ever about Europe's place in the world and about its whole future. Even instinctive integrationists such as the German elite fret that the vision is being swathed in fog by the complexities of Brussels regulation and the struggles of the eurozone. Meanwhile, the lukewarm British commercial pragmatists never really committed themselves to the concept of Europe as an identity at all.

Yet the facts of history have created shared interests and cultural connections that are in the end more important than the differences. We know we are different from Asia; and we are more different from America than we (especially the British) think we are. We have also been reminded of late that Europe's huge neighbour to the east – Russia – has a history and a culture which is quite distinctive and that its identity has a different centre of gravity. In a 21st century world of globalisation and great powers – a century in some ways not so very different from the 19th-century world which was also one of globalisation and great powers – Europe needs to define and discover its common identity.

The 21st century is not going to be Europe's age. Europe is now in long-term relative decline, both politically and economically. It is no longer the energetic, ambitious and aggressive continent it was when the Portuguese, the Spanish, the Dutch, the French and the British set out over the oceans to plunder, trade and colonise. Europe also is no longer the continent whose technical brilliance the Chinese emperor Qianlong so unwisely spurned when Lord Macartney sought to open commercial dealings with China in 1793. It is no longer the continent where an aggressive Germany sought to settle and Germanise vast tracts of Slav land to the east and unleashed a campaign of unbelievable brutality in pursuit of that goal. And it is no longer the frontline of a Cold War between two superpowers with the capacity to destroy each other and everyone else many times over. Europe has retreated from being the self-defined centre of the world to being what it had been before the 15th century – a corner of the Eurasian land mass. At that time it was backward in comparison either with the sophistication of China (with which it had very little contact) or with the intellectual prowess of the Muslim world (which has left its visible European imprint in the glories of Andalusia). That is not true today: modern Europe is of course one of the most sophisticated and prosperous societies on the planet. But the question about how it can sustain its prosperity and its intellectual stature in an age when the centre of gravity has moved away from it – the question about what it has to offer and on what basis it can expect to retain its influence – is becoming more and more insistent.

The political decline of Europe has been under way remorselessly for a hundred years. All the European powers have lost the empires they acquired with varying degrees of intention and brutality. The record of imperialism is very mixed: the French and the British saw themselves at least partly as civilisers, not just as colonisers and competitors in the unseemly scramble for Africa. But each of the major colonisers has something to be profoundly ashamed of, and which bedevils key relationships with other nations and cultures to this day. For the French it is the tragedy of Algeria, where colonisation and decolonisation was brutal and bloody to a degree that few French people have truly absorbed: the war of independence in the 1950s cost several hundred thousand Algerian lives. For the British, the Bengal famine of 1943 lies – or should lie – on the national conscience; so should the Natives Land Act of 1913 which laid the basis for apartheid in South Africa; and the opium wars of the 19th century are a huge national disgrace which the Chinese do not forget, even if the British prefer not to remember (and, when confronted with the facts, to assume it is all just past history with no relevance to the present). For the Germans, the eastern colonisation project (with its associated and systematic genocide of Jews and massive slaughter of Slavs) was of course in an unspeakable class of its own – although the uncomfortable truth is that they have been more honest with themselves about the facts than either the French or the British.

The post-war settlement initially assumed that nothing had changed. Britain and France as victorious allies and imperial powers gained permanent seats with veto rights on the United Nations Security Council. Churchill had famously proclaimed in 1943 that he had not become the King's First Minister in order to preside over the dissolution of the British Empire. Later, Charles de Gaulle equally publicly committed himself to the defence of *Algérie française*. And even though both countries gave those empires up over the following decades, both meant to retain enough independent hard power to protect their vital interests on the world stage. Both developed independent nuclear deterrents. Both too lay claim to significant soft power based on the legacy of their imperialist pasts – in the context of such mechanisms as the Francophonie and the Commonwealth.

There is considerable substance in this soft power – although this very fact carries its own dangers, because it means that both countries tend to underestimate the residual resentment left by their imperialist ventures. But no delusions can remain about the decline of their hard power and of their political ability to use it. Neither any longer has the strength or the mass to sustain a significant military campaign alone. Britain could no longer recapture the Falklands, as it successfully did in 1982. And it is now doubtful whether either country could get away with major military action other than as part of some form of internationally endorsed campaign (except perhaps in a former colony, on a limited basis and by appropriate invitation – as the British did in Sierra Leone in 2000 or the French did in Mali in 2013).

Meanwhile, the Germans remain viscerally unwilling to project their power militarily. Their refusal to vote for air strikes in Libya in the UN Security Council in 2011 was emblematic. They have since taken the leading role in Europe's engagement with the Ukraine crisis: but this has been possible only because no one believes that military action can be part of the response. Nothing demonstrates the enduring German sensitivity about the past more clearly than this neuralgia about hard power – graphically underlined by sharp contrast between the humdrum status of the Bundeswehr and the prewar aura of the Wehrmacht.

But at no point in the decades after the war has the decline of the British and the French and the refusal of the Germans been compensated by the development at the European level of any credible collective ability to project independent hard power. Not since the European Defence Community project (which the British had blessed but had no intention of joining) was voted down by the French National Assembly in 1954 has there been any serious attempt to resurrect such a concept. Looking forward, it is clear that Europe does not even want to do so. Nor is there any sign of a collective European wish to resolve the increasingly archaic position of the French and the British at the United Nations Security Council in favour of a European solution, let alone of the French or the British themselves taking any such initiative.

Recent years have seen the first coherent efforts to project a European collective presence in the geopolitical arena, through the engagement of the still relatively new External Action Service of the EU[2] – mainly in its own backyard and by extension into its broader hinterland (in, for example, the delicate negotiations with Iran over its nuclear capabilities). The EU has also joined international sanctions programmes against a number of pariah states over the years. But almost nobody expects (or even wants) all this to develop into a degree of activity which diminishes the primacy of individual member states' foreign policy. It is striking that in the case of the Ukraine, it is one member state – Germany – which has led and, in effect, determined the European response to Russia's actions. The truth is that nobody expects the political decline of the European nations to be offset by a stronger European geopolitical identity, not even necessarily in its own neighbourhood.

Europe is also in relative decline as an economic force, not just as a locus of political power. Having led the world during the first industrial revolution of the 19th century, it then saw the centre of gravity shift away from it across the Atlantic from the beginning of the 20th century and especially after the First World War. After the massive destruction of the Second World War, the United States was firmly ensconced as the overwhelmingly dominant economic power. At least this meant that (Western) Europe could position itself as part of a transatlantic relationship with shared interests, a common commitment to democracy, and – up to a point – a common economic approach. As a result, Western Europe's economy grew rapidly for a while as it recovered from devastation, bringing the people of Europe a degree of widespread prosperity they had never known before.

But this proved to be only an interlude. For since the epochal year of 1989, the rise of Asia has driven a new and historic shift of the centre of global economic gravity, this time to the east. Growth rates have risen in all the continents once dominated by the European powers. But above all, this is an Asian story. So successful has Asia been in the last three decades that its insatiable demand for resources and markets has driven growth in the Middle East, in Latin America and latterly in Africa. At the centre of this remarkable phenomenon is the reemergence of China as a great power – now the largest exporter in the world and asserting its right to a place in the sun. But it is not only a Chinese story: the other Asian behemoth – India – is lumbering forward too, not at the determined and driven pace China has achieved in recent decades, but nevertheless at rates that are almost doubling its economy every decade. Others too, from the large and diverse (Indonesia) to the small and compact (Singapore) are at various stages of what is by historical standards globally an astonishingly rapid transformation.

Astonishingly rapid, yes. But not fundamentally different from the earlier experience of the Europeans. As they modernise, all countries urbanise; there is no exception to this rule. Britain's 19th century industrialisation moved the country from being 80 percent rural to 80 percent urban in less than a century. China is achieving the same effect more quickly – but it is presently no more than about half way through the change. India has further to go. There will be bumps along this road, but the best central forecast is that most Asian countries (and indeed, most of the emerging markets of the world) will continue to grow rapidly for another generation, both by their own historical standards and in stark contrast with the sluggishness in the old economies of Europe.

Europe will – inevitably – continue to lose market share as a result of all this. That has been the fate of all the early developers, including both the United States and Japan. Loss of market share is the result of a historic reversion to the norm. Before the 19th century, the world's economic output was never far from subsistence level: so a country's share of global output was roughly in proportion to its share of world population. Then as now, China had the largest population in the world – and, as late as about 1820, China had the world's largest economy.

That changed with the onset of the industrial revolution. For the first time in human history, it enabled some economies to produce consistently above subsistence level, thus creating a gap between the two ratios (Malthus was wrong – at least once industrialisation and urbanisation had begun to destroy older social structures[3]). First the Europeans, then the Americans, and later the Japanese, thus achieved enormous increases in world market share. At the peak of their relative outperformance, these developed countries represented less than a fifth of the world's population, but created around three quarters of world GDP.

The gap is now closing again as not only China but country after country in Asia (and elsewhere in the emerging world) start to catch up with the standards of living which Europeans have come to take for granted. Within ten years or so, on present trends, China may well be the world's largest economy again: and that is just a milestone – eventually China will be by far the largest economy in the world. This great convergence, with all that it implies, is the most important fact about the first half of the 21st century.

So even if all had gone well for the Europeans, they would have had to become used to dealing with major new actors on the world stage. But in fact the weakness of European performance has exacerbated the change. This is partly due to the costs and rigidities of its social market economic model (summed up in Chancellor Merkel's famous comment that Europe has 7% of the world's population, 25% of its output and 50% of its social spending), partly to the extreme stress within the eurozone, and partly to the global financial and economic crisis which was unleashed in 2007/8. This hit the Europeans more badly than the Asians (whose balance sheets had been repaired in the wake of the Asian crisis ten years before). So the crisis has, if anything, accelerated the historic shift towards the east.

Europe is left struggling to find a secure foothold in a global marketplace which is becoming more and more interwoven – where the US remains by far the world's largest military power as well as a formidably versatile, inventive and dynamic economy, and where Europe's ever more sophisticated eastern competitors have in several cases already passed the stage of competing simply on the basis of large pools of cheap labour.

The Asians look at Europe and see a large and prosperous market with some attractive investment opportunities. But they also see a jaded and insecure society that has – to quote the famous, and still devastatingly accurate, remark by an erstwhile American Secretary of State about the British (but generalising it to apply to the Europeans as a whole) – lost its empires and not yet found a role.[4] One Chinese diplomat somewhat sardonically summed up what Europe has to offer to the modern world as 'museums and education'. In the limit, it is as if the fate of modern Europe, obsessed as it is with its modern Greek problem, will echo that of ancient Greece. Classical Greece is remembered now for its literature, its philosophy, its democratic experiments, its internecine warfare, and an empire which expanded far and wide before fragmenting and then being overwhelmed by newer, more dynamic powers – Romans, Arabs, Turks. Does such a fate await Europe now?

Meanwhile, the US knows that the Europeans are increasingly poorly equipped junior partners in NATO and less likely than ever to join any 'coalition of the willing' in the use of hard power. But since the demise of the Soviet empire, Europe is no longer a major focus of strategic concern for the Americans anyway. So will the Europeans come to be seen in their eyes as what Canada and Australia are: broadly reliable friends – the kind of middle-class neighbours you like to have around, the kind who have some common interests and are like minded in many ways – but whom you wouldn't count on for too much?

China's mood is in some ways reminiscent of Germany's in the late 19th century: conscious that its time has come and determined to be taken seriously by the existing occupants of the world stage; and burning with not-so-ancient grievances against some of those occupants (for Germany then it was France: for China now it is Japan in particular – but also

the Opium wars, the Boxer Rebellion, and European duplic-
ity over Shandong). It is also, like Germany then, ready to
compete militarily with the leading military power (now, as
then, through an aggressive naval build up).

China and the United States are increasingly wary of each
other. As they watch each other, both China and the US recognise what is happening and know that Europe is losing its
historical significance. They know that if there were moments
in the last century when Europe might have come together
in a stronger and more effective union, those moments have
passed and will not recur. What if a real United States of
Europe had arisen from the ashes after 1945 – as imagined
by Churchill in his famous Zürich speech of 1946 (although
Churchill had no intention that Britain itself should actually
join such a union)? What if the European Defence Community had not been stillborn? And what if the Treaty of Lisbon
had provided for a directly elected President of the European
Union? None of these things happened, and realists would
certainly argue that the conditions were never there for such
radical breaks with the past. That is as may be, but the result
is clear: Europe's response to its diminished position on
the world stage, to the new economic competition it faces
around the globe, and to the challenges all this implies for its
own evolution, has been underwhelming.

The Europeans: caught in the headlights?

The question is therefore about the implications of all this for the nature of Europe, for its identity. Is it, after all, basically nothing more than a series of small and medium-sized economies with varying strengths and weaknesses, all seeking to swim in the currents of the global economic mainstream and none of them big enough to have significant geopolitical influence? This is precisely the formula of the British eurosceptics, for example, who imagine that a Britain freed from the shackles of Europe could negotiate its own terms of trade with the rest of the world and who equate such freedom with strength (they can also sometimes be heard to muse about a renewed and familial relationship with the Commonwealth as if that were a realistic alternative economic strategy to EU membership).

Or is there more to it than that? Does Europe have a common identity which differentiates it from America and from Asia, and which gives it something distinctive to offer to the 21st century? And if so, how will its people recognise and express that common identity? What does it mean – both in the depths of self-awareness and in practice – to be a European?

Europe's effort to assert such an identity has been hobbled, first, by the complexity of a Union which now has 28 member states and will have well over 30 within the next 20 years or so. Yet its governance was basically designed for a community of less than half that size, with far less disparity of wealth and development than is now the case. Its cumbersome and dysfunctional structure cries out for reform; but the process of building consensus for change is painfully slow. It is often said of democratic politics that radical reform is only triggered by crises. In the EU's case the opposite seems to have happened: the stress caused in the eurozone by the economic and financial crisis has sapped the energy for more fundamental reform of the system.

It is not that nothing is happening. The new Commission which took office in November 2014 began work with a new and much more rational division of policy portfolios, together with new strategic priorities well-attuned to the challenge of achieving growth and job creation in the EU, and a major new impetus behind regulatory simplification and efficiency (driven by a powerful new First Vice President with what is effectively a Chief Operating Officer brief).[5] The eurozone group has put in place the banking union and the stabilisation mechanisms needed to underpin the currency. And the European Central Bank has shown itself to be increasingly effective in macroeconomic management in the face of sustained slow growth and deflationary risks. All of this is clearly welcome.

But the task ahead is daunting, if Europe is to achieve the dynamism and flexibility needed to compete against the Asians and the Americans and create jobs for its youth. One measure of the size of the mountain it has to climb is the state of the Single Market (Europe's other flagship economic project alongside the single currency). The last few decades have seen significant progress in creating a genuine and broad based single market in goods across the face of the Union (you can sell the same car anywhere in 28 markets with no modifications – other than which side to put the steering wheel – because of the existence of uniform regulations across the whole Union). But the services sectors (which represent more than three quarters of European output) are riddled with local and national non-tariff barriers. Professional qualifications and regulations differ widely from one jurisdiction to another, and affect everything from architectural and legal services to selling books or insurance products. Removing those is proving to be trench warfare against battalions of special interests across the EU. And the last few years have posed a whole new challenge in implementing a single European market – the rise of online trading and the need to allow borderless growth of such businesses so that they can fulfil their potential. Overall, the truth is that Europe has been making crabwise improvements which are a long way short of achieving the degree of efficiency and flexibility it needs in the face of the global challenge – while the rest of the world has not been standing still.

So governance remains cumbersome and opaque, growth is muted, and structural unemployment – especially amongst the young – remains high. It is perhaps, therefore, no surprise that there is widespread though inchoate disaffection amongst Europe's citizens for the 'real existing' Europe (to borrow a phrase coined by East German critics of the actual outworking of socialism in their Marxist paradise). The original vision of the founders of what is now the EU has given way, as far as many of its citizens are concerned, to a confused sense of the complexity and unresponsiveness of it all. They want to be assured of a predictable continuity which is not in fact available. At the same time they feel very distant from the corridors of power. This public mood has been exacerbated by the absence of any strong and clear leadership based on a real democratic mandate at the Union level, ready to set out the right blend of vision and home truths about Europe's place in this changing world.

There is, in short, little loyalty to – little love of or pride in – the institutions which represent Europe, and almost nothing that could be described as fervent European patriotism. The absence of any widespread European patriotism contrasts sharply with both the American and the Chinese view of the world and of themselves (and indeed with the rising assertiveness of India). American homes often have a Stars and Stripes flying from a flagpole on their front lawn; very few European homes indeed fly the European flag, though many of course brandish their national flag at the time of European or World Cup football matches. Meanwhile, Chinese patriotism (and sometimes xenophobia) are an inescapable feature of the lively and influential Chinese blogosphere. There is no European equivalent.

Why the contrast? Partly because the Europeans seem to disdain such overt displays of patriotic fervour other than when defanged in the context of sport. Partly because of the way their history has desacralised and discredited nationalist patriotism. But more deeply because it directly reflects a fundamental uncertainty about their own identity as Europeans. This identity crisis in Europe has been exacerbated by the rise of Asia. Admiration for the extraordinary achievements of modern Asia has brought Europe's own uncertainties about its place in the world and about its values into sharp relief. So this admiration is tinged with nervousness. Europeans are unsettled by the fear that the Asians will challenge and eventually overtake them; no area of activity is free from the competitive threat from this huge reservoir of human talent.

For Asia is no longer just a limitless supply of hardworking cheap labour. Europeans fear that Asian technical brilliance may overwhelm them in the very areas of strength they have prided themselves on. In fact, for several decades now, the Europeans have been fighting a rearguard action in their own minds. Ever since the Japanese (and then the Koreans, the Taiwanese, Hong Kong and Singapore, now China, and increasingly other South East Asians) began to take on the West at their own game – making transistors, cars, televisions, ships and other such wares that were initially derided as cheap, poorly designed would-be competitors of the real European thing – they have convinced themselves that there is always a remaining comparative advantage to which they can retreat. Whether it was primary research as opposed to 'mere engineering', or education which stressed lateral thinking as opposed to 'mere rote learning', or artistic creativity as opposed to 'mere excellence in performance', or elegance and originality of design as opposed to imitation and functionalism, the Europeans have wanted to hang on to something distinctive that would not be swamped by the rising tide. But no: with every passing year it becomes ever clearer that there are no European heights that the Asians will not eventually scale. The Americans face the same challenge, of course, but the Europeans ruefully recognise how the much greater inventiveness, drive and flexibility of the American society and economy has enabled them to continue to renew themselves in the most unpredictable ways. No European country or company has been able to match the spectacular successes of Silicon Valley, which few had even heard of at the time of the fall of the Berlin Wall.

All of this is nurturing a sense of inferiority and uncertainty about who we Europeans really are. Many are beguiled by, for example, Singaporean and Chinese intellectuals who argue that their societies are more socially integrated, less individualist, more long term in their orientation – and yes, more patriotic – than the selfish, short-termist societies of the Western democracies. Despite this critique, however, they have at least a grudging respect for America because of its sheer power. That respect does not extend to Europe.

Many of Europe's elites, both in the public sector and in business, secretly – or indeed openly – agree with this Asian critique of their own societies. And almost every European business with any significant international strategy intones a mantra that says 'go east'. There is widespread respect, in short, for this Asian special path.

Not that this Asian special path is any less materialistic in its aspirations, judging by the shape of emerging middle-class demand throughout the region. From McDonalds to Johnnie Walker, Mercedes and Jaguar, to pop music and to branded fashion accessories, their appetite for the paraphernalia of Western life seems limitless. As for the cultural authenticity and creativity that Asian societies with such long and rich traditions might have been expected to project, the truth is rather that there has been a wholesale rush towards kitsch and glitz. In particular, what has been done to the ancient cities of Asia in the name of modern development is in many cases tragic. Future generations will surely curse all the destruction – the loss of so much of the old Beijing, for example, and comparable losses in so many of the big cities of the new Asia.

So we could well ask of Asia's presumed special path: how real is it? And how durable, how deeply rooted in the cultural identity of their societies? Indeed, it is perfectly clear that the leadership in more and more Asian societies is becoming anxious about the spiritual vacuum being created in the hell-for-leather rush towards modernisation. The Chinese authorities, notably, worry publicly about the values of a new generation of urban middle classes who have been so recently uprooted from traditional rural social and family structures and are no longer imbued with the classic Confucian ethos of harmony and social order.

But what about Europe? Even as some of the 21st century's most important new challengers lay claim to their own new special path, Europeans agonise about how they are to make their way in this new world. Is there some level at which there are fundamental commonalities, shared by 28 different member states, which give them a common vision of their place in the world? Is there, in other words, a European identity?

Identity in variety?

All European history seems to cry out that the answer is no. There are surely just too many differences – of language, of religion, of culture? These differences have been deeply embedded by the facts of history, they are hard to eradicate or gloss over, and they therefore seem to militate against the emergence of any real European loyalty. The differences amount to wholly distinct ways of life. No one could mistake Palermo for Stockholm, or Athens for Galway. The language, the appearance, the atmosphere, the style of living are so fundamentally different. This variety is thrown into relief all the more clearly by the sharp contrast with the broad and bland similarity between American cities from one end of the country to the other – the physical manifestation of the famous American melting pot.

But could it be argued that there is indeed a European identity and that this very variety is itself a crucial element in that identity – that it is precisely that rich, colourful kaleidoscope which makes Europe what it is?

Is this real? Can it really be the basis of an identity? No: because identity is not just about what might be called traditional 'local colour' – Alpine horns versus bagpipes, paella versus roast beef and Yorkshire pudding, beer versus wine, and so forth. If it were, the differences would by now have ceased to matter as more and more of everything is obtainable everywhere. Nor is it about differences in urban behaviour which are much more recent in origin: the punctilious British driver stopping for a pedestrian on a zebra crossing unlike the oblivious French driver; or the dutiful German pedestrian waiting to cross until the pedestrian light turns green, even if there is no car (or policeman) in sight. Nor again is it just about cultural differences – how the major Christian festivals are celebrated, for example. For the Germans no Christmas is culturally complete without Bach's Christmas Oratorio, whilst for the English it is the Christmas carol service which brings back the memories of childhood – and Holy Week in Spain is an utterly distinctive and intense community drama. Such differences (and there are many others amongst the European regions) are easy to spot, but they are hardly the stuff of which barriers to shared identity are made. (It is, however, noteworthy that there is no European equivalent to the unifying importance of Thanksgiving and its rituals to Americans – or of the lunar New Year to the Chinese.)

But language and history – including deep history (the kind of history which colours the attitudes of today, even when most individuals are aware of it only through simplifying myths) – are another matter. European nations were to a large extent formed by language. The standardisation of French based on its northern dialect accompanied the extension of Paris-based French royal power through more and more of what is now the French state – with the eclipse of a culturally separate south and of the Burgundian domains. The Hundred Years War in the 14th and 15th centuries helped forge a national identity in both France and England, and it is surely no coincidence that it was also the time when English re-emerged from the shadows as the language not just of the peasantry but of an aristocratic elite which had spoken French for the previous 300 years. The German and Italian identities were rooted even more firmly in their languages, in the absence for many centuries of a national political identity. For Germany, it was Martin Luther's translation of the Bible into High German that drove the standardisation of the German language – which in turn became the expression and vehicle for the rising German self-awareness of the 18th and 19th centuries. For Italy, the formative influence was Dante's brilliant use of the vernacular Italian he knew.

In fact, the crystallisation of national languages was both cause and effect of a flourishing of literature, which in turn contributed to a growing sense of national identity. Dante, Shakespeare, Cervantes, Racine and Goethe became part of the European patrimony: their themes have inspired others across the linguistic barriers (and in the worlds of European art and music). But in the first instance they were and are emblems of their own linguistic cultures. Language history therefore matters.

So important is language that the changing geography of language changes identity. Prague became a Czech speaking city in just a generation as a result of Czech immigration into the city in the late 19th century, having been for centuries the German-speaking seat of one of the Electors of the Holy Roman Empire of the German Nation. Its identity – and eventually its nationality – thus changed forever. By the time Kafka was writing there in the early 20th century, he was a member of a (Jewish) minority in a (German speaking) minority in a Czech city.

The contrast with both America and China is striking. America the melting pot was formed by the English language. First generation immigrants might speak it imperfectly for the rest of their lives, and would use their native tongue at home and in their immigrant communities. But the second and third generations became native English speakers – and gradually melted into the new American culture so completely that only their surnames betrayed where their ancestors had come from (even if many continued to take pride in those ancestral connections). China's story is completely different, and yet in the end the result is the same. China was not a land of immigrants, in fact it is one of the most ethnically homogeneous countries in the world. But it was a vast land of people who spoke different languages (albeit etymologically related). Its bond was its ideographical script, which enabled a literate society to communicate and strengthen its identity – and which in turn, when the time came under the People's Republic, facilitated the deliberate spreading of Mandarin Chinese as a true, unifying national language.

Europe has had no such unifying language. Latin was for centuries the language which enabled scholars to communicate freely across ordinary linguistic barriers, and French became the diplomatic lingua franca in the 18th century. English is of course now Europe's diplomatic, commercial and intellectual lingua franca, as it is that of the world at large. But a common language of policy, commerce and science is a very different thing from the language of common life and shared identity. Europe remains a linguistic patchwork, with all that means for cultural diversity and the proliferation of identities.

Not that language has ever been the only basis for aware-
ness of identity in Europe: and nor is a shared language evidence of – let alone a guarantee of – a common identity.
Cultural identity is moulded by other powerful influences
– notably religion, of course. And political identity has
fractured in several cases despite a common language. The
British suppression of the Irish language was largely successful (even if the mythic power of the Irish language lives on),
but they certainly did not succeed in eliminating the Irish
aspiration for autonomy and then independence (of which
more later). Conversely, religious differences and political history can overwhelm linguistic commonality, as the
Dutch/Flemish speakers of The Netherlands and Belgium
can attest. In very different circumstances, the same result
is evident in the case of Austria: the German speakers of
Austria developed a clearly separate national identity as Austrians – rather than as Austrian Germans or German Austrians – in the space of a few decades after the Second World
War, just as the German speakers of the Swiss Alps had done
several centuries before.

So language was never the only cause of either the fragmentation of the European identity or of the consolidation
of national identities. Latin was not simply elbowed out by
the newly standardised national languages. There was something else afoot: the history of beliefs and ideas matters.
The decline of Latin was one of the outworkings of the
destruction of European Christian unity brought about by
the Reformation (or, perhaps better, Reformations) which
swept through Europe in the 16th century and ushered in
more than a century of turmoil and war. The tangled stories

of reformation and national assertion in various European countries helped drive the language cultures of Europe apart. The distinctive English settlement; the Dutch Protestant struggle against their Spanish overlords; the savagery of the religious wars in Germany in the 16th century followed by the catastrophe of the Thirty Years War in the 17th – all this and much else struck at the roots of European identity.

Its after-effects reverberated for centuries and have not completely disappeared even today, long after we have forgotten the passions which generated so much fury. In most cases, countries ended up as either Catholic or, in one form or another, Protestant. But one – the Spanish Netherlands – was split apart into what became the Belgium and The Netherlands that we now know. And the largest of all – the German lands of the Holy Roman Empire – were fractured along confessional lines that bedevilled the subsequent journey of unification and complicated the quest for a stable German identity.

Again, this European experience and its impact are distinctive. America imported all the European schisms (as well as inventing some of its own). But religious differences never threatened the integrity of its identity and no one was ever defined as non-American because of their religion (though this is not to say that no one was ever persecuted or socially ostracised because of their religion; and of course the different issue of race – first in the struggle over slavery and then in that for civil rights – very nearly tore the country apart). China's experience has been different again: for centuries the dominant Confucian ethos, with its non-theistic metaphysics and its lack of interest in theological dogmatics, seemed to leave no room for religious passion and turmoil. The exceptional – and almost unbelievably violent – Tai Ping rebellion of the 1850/60s, had its bizarre religious background in a peculiar Christian heresy. The only other period in recent centuries when China has known violent upheaval triggered by religion – or rather, its 20th-century ideological equivalent, Maoism – was that of the Cultural Revolution. This too had its distant ancestry in European millenarianism. But neither episode – terrible though they both were – did permanent damage to the national self-understanding. In the new dispensation ushered in by Deng Xiao Ping, Confucian values are again revered and are as quietly powerful as ever in moulding the national identity.

In short, both America and China have been through existential crises in the last two centuries: but in neither case has this in the last analysis fractured their identity. Europe, by contrast, destroyed the unity of Christendom and tore itself apart. Nationalism was the eventual winner, and the impact on the European identity was devastating. Come 1945, the question was whether it could ever recover.

Enlightenment or enlightenments?
The birth of a new European identity?

It is perhaps debatable whether European religious reformation needed to take the explosive form that it did. Historical 'what ifs' are always tempting. What if, for example, Martin Luther had been received by the young and new Emperor Charles V more sympathetically at the Diet of Worms in 1521? European Christendom would certainly have had to change, but could it have remained intact? Charles V, Holy Roman Emperor and King of Spain and all its domains, was the sovereign who came closer to embodying Christendom than any other before or after. His motto *Plus Ultra* ('further beyond'), emblazoned against an image of the Pillars of Hercules, conveyed a sense of the limitless power of Christendom as it spread out from Spain into the New World – but at just the moment in history when its spiritual integrity was under existential threat.

And not only its spiritual integrity. For even if the answer is yes – even if Charles V could have sponsored reform from within such that schism could have been averted – something other than theological dispute was fermenting in European intellectual circles by then. A new intellectual curiosity was beginning to eat away at the metaphysical certainties and intellectual integrity of Christendom, with its fusion of Christian theology and Greek classical wisdom whose finest exponent had been the brilliant Thomas Aquinas. The new world that was coming into view was not only that of Columbus: it was that of Galileo, whose *'mente concipio'* ('I conceive with my (own) mind') was an assertion of the right to experiment and explore without necessarily accepting any inherited preconceptions. It was the beginning of a journey of the mind which would lead all the way to Darwin. The old world-view was fragmenting as the Renaissance gathered momentum: the challenge to the old metaphysical certainties was inevitable.

But there was a question: could the new spirit of rationalist enlightenment replace the integrated world-view of Christendom with another basis for a common European identity?

The origins of the European Enlightenment are complex. The spirit of Columbus and Galileo was clearly at its root. But the Christian humanism of a figure such as Erasmus – the influential Catholic priest, ecclesiastical and social reformer, and scholar of the foundational texts of Christian thought – played a crucial role too. Born in the port city of Rotterdam (where an openness to all comers was somehow part of the atmosphere), he travelled widely and died in Basel. He was in communication with Luther but refused to be lured by his separatism, and spent his life arguing for reform from within the system. He wrote all his works in Latin to ensure the widest possible exchange of ideas. Erasmus is the archetype of the European citizen, reared in a Christian tradition which had drawn inspiration from classical Greek wisdom and Roman civilisation as well as being rooted in the world of Jewish monotheism. He believed in the power of reasoned argument (not just for ecclesiastical reform but, by extension, in policy formation generally) and in the overwhelming importance of preserving religious (and therefore cultural) unity. Not for nothing did the EU name its highly valued programme of supporting students to study in other member countries after this remarkable and irenic figure.

But what Erasmus represented did not prevail on the European stage over the 400-year span from his death until the disasters of the 20th century. Christendom broke apart and national consciousness was on the rise everywhere. The respect for reason which was the essence of the intellectual movement of the Enlightenment was never going to fill the vacuum left by a shared institutional faith: it was never going to compete successfully with the fissiparous power of nationalism.

Indeed, the Enlightenment itself evolved in an increasingly fragmented European intellectual atmosphere – so that it is arguably misleading to speak of it as a uniform movement of the European spirit. In particular, enlightenment as it developed in the three leading countries of Europe took on markedly different tones, reflecting and moulding three differing world-views. These differences have left their imprint on the self-understanding – the identity – of these three countries to this day.

The British are deeply imbued with a pragmatism which is very long standing. The religious settlement reached under the Tudors is a classic – and perhaps even foundational – case in point. Notoriously, Henry VIII declared himself the head of the church, not out of theological conviction but for reasons of state (the need to produce a male heir). Under his son Edward VI and then his elder daughter Mary, the policy first swung abruptly to a more thoroughgoing Protestantism and then back to reinstated Catholicism, before reaching an enduring Anglican solution under Elizabeth. This solution bears all the hallmarks of that propensity which admirers call pragmatism and detractors call fudge. When confronted with two versions of the words of administration in the Communion service – the one more Catholic, the other more Calvinist in implication – Elizabeth simply had the drafters put both together in a single paragraph. The formula is still in use in the modern Anglican liturgy.[6]

This tendency has continued to manifest itself in British intellectual and public life to this day. The British philosophical tradition embodies an individualism which owes its origins to John Locke – the progenitor of liberalism – and to the sceptical empiricism of David Hume (who denied that it was possible to say anything absolute about experience based on a priori reasoning). It is a tradition which does not encourage metaphysical speculation, or indeed any form of philosophical 'system'. If it has a world-view, it is a view which doesn't attempt to see beyond the horizon of experience and which crosses one bridge at a time. This is the world of Adam Smith, of enlightened self-interest and of utilitarianism. This is also the world-view which underlies the British approach to governance and constitutional reform, as it has been played out over the centuries. Political evolution in Britain has typically been incrementalist, opportunist and often almost accidental – as attested by a long series of examples from Disraeli's Second Reform Act, through repeated efforts to reform the House of Lords, and to the establishment of national parliaments, a London mayoralty and the Supreme Court under the Blair government.

One way or another, the pragmatism of the British has been enough to fend off revolution (an outcome we now tend to take for granted, but which was not so obvious even as late as the middle of the 20th century). By stark contrast, of course, the French produced a revolution which was the biggest and most complex social explosion Europe had ever known. Famously, the Chinese Communist leader Zhou En Lai, when asked almost two centuries later about its consequences, is alleged to have replied that it was too soon to tell. It was part chaos and terror, part human and social engineering on an unprecedented scale. And its aftermath has revealed (and created?) two very different aspects of the French identity. To this day, the French establishment has a more elevated view than the British of the role of the state in social development, more confidence in the leadership of a meritocratic elite, and more porous borders between the private and public spheres. And on the other hand, the French are notoriously ready to turn out on the streets in protest against government. A rationalism which has its ancestor in the comprehensiveness of the Napoleonic programme (and perhaps also in the centralising absolutism of Louis XIV) – together with an appetite for demonstrations which is a distant echo of the original upheaval with its elemental violence. This is the enduring contest within the French identity. *Étatisme* confronted by the barricades.

Nurturing the *étatisme* is the continuing and profound influence of the presiding genius of French thought. For Descartes, the human self has an innate rationality which means that it can approach experience with an a priori conceptual logic. This assertion of the power of the intellect over experience was what Hume was reacting against: his scepticism was forged precisely in opposition to this elevated view of the status of human reason. If the British propensity for fudge is underpinned by a pragmatic philosophical empiricism, the French propensity for elitist social engineering is equally clearly based on Cartesian first principles. It was a tradition nurtured by the *philosophes* of the 18th century – that remarkable group of French thinkers who became known simply as the *Lumières*. French intellectuals, in contrast to the British, evolved a systematic approach to the world – even if they were no more interested in metaphysics than their deistic British counterparts.

The outworkings are visible in French public life today: in the rational consistency of the French economic and social model, in the comprehensive planning of the French national infrastructure, in the civil code, in the metric system which was promulgated in the early years of the Revolution, in the zeal of the Académie Française for preserving the purity of the French language – and in much else besides. Where British pragmatism can be flexible to the point of being haphazard and drifting, French rationalism can be consistent to the point of being rigid and brittle. It is no coincidence that whilst Britain has had one endlessly shifting and unclearly defined constitution, France has had five republics (as well as two empires and a monarchy) in the two centuries since the Revolution. But it is probably also the most efficient (though certainly not the lowest cost) state in Europe. When the Channel Tunnel opened in 1994, the French already had a high-speed rail link to Paris: it took the British another nine years to complete the connection to London. France established its national hub airport in the right place in the 1970s; Britain's hub airport is in the wrong place without adequate capacity, and there is still no finally agreed way forward.

And Germany? Wasn't it always a complicated blend of duty and discipline, but also of metaphysics and romanticism – the land of all those philosophers, poets and composers? If France is the soil of rationalism and Britain is the home of empiricism and pragmatic utilitarianism, then Germany is the home of metaphysics and systems. "I am therefore I think" – to reverse Descartes's famous dictum – captures one pole of the German psyche, still in evidence in the 21st century.

Germany's culture has been strongly shaped by three towering figures: Luther, Kant and Hegel. Its cultural revolution was unleashed by Martin Luther. Luther saw Christians as living in two realms – that of their spiritual experience of grace and salvation, and that of interaction with others: the interior world and the exterior world. The interior world – this was Luther's great innovation – is an individual, personal one. For him, the decision of faith – the central decision, of both existential and eternal significance – was for the individual alone. Meanwhile, in the exterior world the role of the civil authorities is to maintain peace and the social order, whilst the duty of the subject is to show obedience to the civil authorities. The prince who kept order – by force as necessary – was doing the work of God's kingdom. Without the prince, the world would descend into unavoidable chaos.

This world-view became more and more influential with the rise of Prussia in the 18th century. But it also gave a distinctively German impetus to the Enlightenment. If the French

Enlightenment was more radically revolutionary (and anti-clerical), and the English and Scottish Enlightenments were economic and libertarian, the German Enlightenment was at once more metaphysical and more compatible with absolutism. Its most important figure – Immanuel Kant – was, to use his famous phrase, 'awoken from his dogmatic slumbers' by the challenge of Hume's scepticism.

Kant is undoubtedly the subtlest, profoundest and strongest influence on German thought since Luther. His answer to Luther's question about grace and salvation – that inner realm where each individual makes his or her life choices – was, in effect, yes: you make your own decisions, within the limits of what you can know and in the absence of any metaphysical certainty, about what you believe and how you live. But the question that needed an answer was one about commitment: what could you devote yourself to, in the absence of any demonstrable metaphysical certainties? This might be described as the post-Enlightenment – or post-Lutheran, or post-Kantian – question. It is as pressing today as ever.

Hegel, who should surely stand on almost as prominent a pedestal as Kant, was eclipsed for a time by others – notably Marx. But he has been increasingly recognised in recent decades for what he was: a – or even *the* – fundamental alternative (or counterpoint) to Kant, whose relevance to modern debates about the politics of identity in a globalising world is as profound as ever. Where Kant was sceptical about any metaphysical certainty and immovably focused on the rational, autonomous individual subject, Hegel was on a very different journey. He was not alone in seeking to cut through the veil of perception to an absolute that subsumed the self in a wider, all-embracing whole. This was the quest of the Romantic poets who sought to experience and express that mysterious oneness of everything. But it was Hegel who turned the Absolute into the 'world spirit' which was actualising itself in human history through a phased historical momentum. This was his famous dialectical process of thesis, antithesis and synthesis: for him there was an overall pattern to history. It was not a smooth, gradualist process of continuous improvement but a conflictual process in which evil and suffering would play a necessary part. The individual was not absolute, and the purpose of the individual was realised in serving the wider whole (which, in Hegel's thought, could however bear an uncomfortable resemblance to the actual Prussian state).

Although Hegel's reputation went into decline in the decades after his death, he had unleashed a probably endless debate about the individual, the community, progress, the state and social justice, which has certainly not lost in intensity or relevance in the midst of rapid world-historical change in the 21st century. He saw history as an over-arching process which would culminate in a universality of human experience never before known. He was uniquely German: it is hard to imagine Hegel having flourished in the empiricist world of British thought or in the rationalist Cartesian world of the French.

The question as to how far all this accounts for the Third Reich has produced book after book over the years. The short answer is that it cannot meaningfully be held to have caused the disaster; but that it perhaps created a cultural environment in which the Third Reich was more possible – and, given its occurrence, more terrible and total in its outworkings.

Even now, in the 21st century, the question touches a nerve in the German psyche. As a result, Germany – now the leading economic, and therefore political, force in Europe – is very reluctant to find itself responsible for moulding the European identity (on which more below).

Meanwhile, one thing is certain: the very idea of a common identity and a European special way stirs uneasiness in all three countries. The British, true to their empiricist and pragmatic heritage, dislike grand schemes. They also have a long-standing fear of continental entanglements, seeing themselves as traders with the world at large. The country whose Queen became Empress of India was never likely to see the Continent as its primary sphere of operation. And yet the lesson of 1914 was – or should have been – clear. Neutrality about Europe was not (and is not) an option. Churchill understood this in 1940 when he offered full union with France in its hour of need, but his Zürich speech in 1946 shows that even he did not understand the full implications for Britain's peacetime destiny.

For the French, on the other hand, Cartesian rationalism, and the social and political principles of the French Enlightenment as embodied in the aspirations of the French Revolution, are a precious treasury of wisdom[7]. They therefore have the responsibility to ensure that any integrationist ambitions at the European level reflect their own worldview. After the Second World War, the European project was thus built on the premise of political leadership by France, at a time when the Germans did not want it and the British refused it. Engraved on a statue of de Gaulle at the Rond-Point Champs-Elysées in Paris is a quotation from one of his speeches: '*Il y a un pacte, vingt fois séculaire, entre la grandeur de la France et la liberté du monde'* – 'There is a two thousand year old pact between the greatness of France and the liberty of the world'.

Meanwhile, the deeply metaphysical instincts of Germany mark it out clearly from the other two. The search for the absolute in which all lesser realities are subsumed (or *aufgehoben* – to use the almost untranslatable German word which has connotations of being lifted up, suspended, transcended, absorbed into some greater whole) is a quintessential German quest. The irony is that this German spiritual and philosophical hinterland, as well as its long history of political fragmentation offset by bonds of linguistic and cultural identity, have given it a greater ability than either of the other two countries to perceive the true basis of a European identity for the 21st century. And this in turn explains something whose true nature the British have never understood – the German commitment to European integration in general and to the eurozone in particular.

The inevitable bonds of geography and history

Does all this mean that, just looking at the case of the three largest European countries (quite apart from the others), there are such fundamental differences of worldview, and therefore of identity, that the formation of a coherent and meaningful European identity has no chance of success?

The answer surely has to be no. For the converse is absurd; plainly, the concept of Europe is more than just a geographical designation, and the Europeans have things in common which are not in the end overwhelmed by these differences, important though they undoubtedly are. Even the British know they are different from the Americans, and in general Europeans have become more conscious of those transatlantic differences over the last five decades, after those first heady years of cultural Americanisation after the war. And no one could be under any illusion about the differences between the cultures of Europe and the cultures of Asia.

Europeans are bound together by the facts of geography and the facts of history, both longer term and more recent – a history which includes extensive cultural interaction and enrichment, notwithstanding all the variety of language, literature and thought patterns.

The facts of geography create common interests. Europe's relationship with its huge neighbour to the east has always been fractious; the Cold War has gone forever, but Russia's determination to define a sphere of influence into which the European Union shall not spread has become much more obvious in recent years. The relationship is further complicated by energy politics; Europe is short of energy and strategically dependent on Russia, as well as more generally on sources of supply that are unstable and/or potentially hostile. And while the energy equation may vary significantly amongst European countries, the challenge of creating a green society does not; all face the challenge and it is clear that it would be absurd for each to tackle this task independently. Finally, Europe's immediate neighbourhoods to the south and south-east are a continuous source of demographic pressure and of insecurity, whose tragic impact is increasingly felt throughout the continent. All of this and more binds the Europeans together in a common destiny. To (only slightly) paraphrase the English poet and preacher John Donne, no country is an island, entire of itself.[8]

History also binds Europe – not just recent history but the deeper history of a continent which has been the cradle of so much wisdom and beauty, as well as the theatre of so much destruction. Our sense of history is formed too much by the stories of power and conflict (whether feudal, national or class). At least as important is the unending dialectic of innovation, elaboration, rejection and integration in the world of art, science and ideas. The violence – but also the creativity and the ferment: all this is our inheritance. It is therefore in so many ways a history of tragedy, which lies beneath the peace, unity and prosperity which Europe has so clearly achieved (and which modern Europeans perhaps take too much for granted). All this has created distinctive values – ways of thinking about the world and of doing things – that amount to a shared identity at a deep level of our self-awareness.

China's history too is tragic – but differently. Down the centuries it has known long periods of peace, sophistication, inventiveness and extraordinary cultural flowering (which would have amazed and been the envy of any European visiting the Middle Kingdom in the centuries before the European Renaissance). But it has also known horrendous periods of civil war and chaos, as well as the profound humiliation of its failure to cope with the impact of the modern world in the 19th and the early 20th centuries. Which means that dialogue between Europeans and Chinese whose purpose was the shared exploration of their respective deep histories, their specifics and their commonalities would be immeasurably enriching to both. In both cases, history weighs on the present, whether we like it or not. In both cases it shapes the modern identity.

History does not weigh on America in the same way. America is no longer young enough to be innocent, and it treasures its own past with a care that condescending Europeans find amusing because it is by their standards so recent. But it is still in an important sense the New World which left the old behind. Even now, this is a country of immense space – with a population density much lower than that of crowded old Europe. And somehow that space still translates into a sense of potential: the individual can always move on. The myths of America are onward-looking, forward-looking. This New World is older than it was, and has known the pain of the Civil War, traumatic failure in Vietnam and a sense of dissatisfaction with its more recent and unhappy excursions in the Middle East. But despite its growing recognition that its time as the world's single global superpower is already drawing to a close, America is not a country whose national psyche is overburdened by loss, guilt or shame. America and Europe are different because their history is different; and this means their identities are different.

The differences manifest themselves in thought patterns and priorities, both collective and individual. The differences are often subtle rather than blatant; and we Europeans share much with America. At one level, we are all children of the Enlightenment. We share the values that are common to democracies – values which are all too often taken for granted by those who have never had to live without them and never had to fight for them.

But at another level there are obvious differences in attitudes and outlooks. Americans are more individualistic than the Europeans (even while also being more patriotic). America has had no absolutist or totalitarian past of its own to haunt its nightmares. It also nurtures more pre-Enlightenment thought patterns – notably, the widespread pre-scientific attitude towards evolution and human origins (the legacy of Darwin is still widely contested in America in a way and to a degree unknown in Europe). All in all, the differences are many and some are profound: between the degree of geographical and social mobility; between European and American assumptions about the right of privacy, or about the right way to provide health care in society, or in the law on such matters as capital punishment or gun control; the differences in the extent of religious conviction and of religious observance; or the much greater passion generated in

America than in Europe by debate about abortion. These are all reminders that the centre of gravity of American attitudes is very different from that of a much more secularised Europe. They are also a reminder to the British, who are more apt than other Europeans to overlook these differences, that they in fact have far more in common with their continental neighbours and less with their transatlantic friends than they usually recognise.

The United States of Europe?

So if there are such deep commonalities, despite all the variety not only on the surface but in the thought worlds of the Europeans, how can that be reflected in a European identity – and how can that identity project itself on the world stage of the 21st century?

As we have already noted, Churchill proposed a United States of Europe amidst the ruins of war in 1946. And the notion of combining sovereignty was not new then either. Intriguingly, there is a still earlier version of a (regional) United States in Europe: the proposed United States of Greater Austria. This idea was floated in a fascinating book by a lawyer in a group around Franz Ferdinand, heir apparent to the Austrian throne, in 1906.[9] It envisaged a reconstruction of the Austro-Hungarian empire into a group of 16 national states with a federal structure under a constitutional monarchy. All the issues of population mix that bedevilled the Versailles negotiations after the War are considered methodically in the proposal. Could it have succeeded? We will never know, but it offers a poignant glimpse of an alternative future which might have been realised, had catastrophe not been ushered in with the assassination of Franz Ferdinand on 28 June 1914.

The sober assessment is, however, that such a United States of Greater Austria would not have been sustainable.

The centrifugal forces would surely have been too strong. The differences from the United States of America are significant. First, language politics would have been extremely complex: the book devotes a whole section to the reasons why the federal official language would have to be German but national languages would be used for all state level official business. Any solution to such an emotive question was probably doomed to be either inefficient or unstable or both. America kept it simple; it would have just one national language, English, to be used officially at all levels throughout the Union. (Had America been establishing a Union now, it might have had to resolve this question differently, given the widespread and rapidly growing use of Spanish.)

In any event, America's other big advantage compared with pre-First World War Austria-Hungary was that at the time of the Founding Fathers it was small and new. Thirteen states with a total population of less than four million, two thirds of whom originated from the British Isles, were never going to have to wrestle with the huge political stresses that Franz Ferdinand knew were building up in Austria-Hungary with its diverse population of over 50 million. (And even in these favourable conditions, the Americans only succeeded in establishing the Union by explicitly avoiding confrontation over the issue of slavery – the question which very nearly broke it apart in the next century.)

At the European level today, the complexity is an order of magnitude greater than it was in *fin de siècle* Vienna. But before we conclude too easily that a United States of Europe could have no future: what about India? This, after all, is indeed a country with a vibrant democracy, a rich and colourful cultural diversity, 29 states and 7 union territories, over 40 official languages, and (with the exception of the Kashmiri question) no secessionist risks. If India can manage such a Union successfully, why can't the wealthy Europeans, with all appliances and means to boot, do so as well?

But the answer to this provocative question is clear. First, the new India was not born in peace and consensus but in bitter and violent strife which resulted in the breakaway of a huge area of historic India into Pakistan (and what subsequently became Bangladesh). Secondly, India's development has certainly been slowed down by all this complexity: its famously argumentative democracy, numbingly ponderous bureaucracy and glacial judicial process have cost it what might be called a 'democratic discount' compared with the dramatic performance of China, as a result of which China is now a visibly much more affluent country than India. Thirdly, and most basically, India did not start by having to create the union from scratch: it existed, and had done so for many generations. Holding together what is already an entity is challenge enough – as not only Indian but also American history tell us (and as Austria-Hungary would have discovered). Creating a new United States of Europe on the American or the Indian model out of a large number of separate European entities with their disparate languages and cultures, with their record of conflict internally and externally, and with no history of political unity – this was never a realistic possibility, not even in the aftermath of catastrophe in the 1940s. And certainly not now.

A fragile union of fragile identities?

What we have instead is a European Union which is on a unique journey. It has progressed from an economic starting point, from a coal and steel community through a common market and the European Economic Community to what is now the European Union, through a series of treaties which have continually increased the degree of integration.

The eurozone has enormously complicated this journey. Every crisis in the eurozone has seen the members, led increasingly openly by Germany, grope towards a new degree of integration to make the zone more and more of a stable economic whole, subject to coherent fiscal and financial policy. Many have seen this as drift rather than the pursuit of a clear strategy – with each stage being cobbled together amateurishly like the crew of a leaking ship doing repairs in rough seas. Yet this is to misjudge what is afoot. There is no turning back from this journey. From a technical point of view, the increasing integration of the eurozone is a one way street; but even more fundamentally, it would be existentially impossible – particularly for Germany – to withdraw from a project whose collapse would unravel the whole tissue of European integration which has been woven since 1949. And what is true for Germany is true at least for the founding members of the original European project – the signatories of the original Treaty of Rome – and in all probability for all the other members of the eurozone too. There is an inevitable price to pay for this: painful adjustments in weaker economies and financial support from the stronger ones – both of which are of course deeply unpopular. But they will be paid because there is neither a practical nor an existential alternative.

So what is the ultimate end of the European project? This question exposes the divergences and the fractured identity of Europe. At one end of a spectrum are the British, who would have had the Union be a single market but very little more than that, and who opted out of the eurozone. At the other end are those who see growing political and economic integration on the basis of an increasingly harmonised socio-economic model – with the eurozone at its core – as both inevitable and desirable. To be clear, even the former position involves a strong Union, because full-blooded implementa-tion of a single market requires a lot more integrative lead-ership and management of the European Union as a whole than many British eurosceptics would want. But the differ-ence between the two ends of the spectrum is nevertheless a wide one: is Europe little more than a trade bloc, or is it indeed a project of increasing political cohesion which will converge in the end towards something that is more like a United States of Europe?

The truth is that neither of these alternative ends of the spectrum is an adequate description – either of the Union as it is actually evolving or of the expectations (however incho-ate) of the broad majority of the Union's citizens. What-ever the emerging European identity is, neither captures it. For the reality is clearly something in between – something sui generis: an evolving set of arrangements for governance and management which recognises both a wider commonality and specific identities. There is nothing quite like it anywhere in the world today. It is of course hard to define, and begs a whole series of questions about how it should actually work. What kinds of relationships between member states or regions does this entail? What should the balance be between centralising, regionalising and localising tendencies? How can the democratic process work to express the public will effectively at all levels – Union, member state, region, local? And can this emerging Europe ever win the real loyalty of its people? – which is a question about identity, not just about democratic processes.

Identity is always a composite. It can have many elements: geography, history, culture, language, common interests, and the way societies govern themselves. No single element is necessary to it (the Jews throughout most of their history had no geographic identity, for example, and the Swiss have no language in common). And no single element is sufficient for it (language alone does not ensure a common identity amongst English or Spanish speakers). Sometimes these sources of identity – notably history – can be problematic; but they cannot be avoided, as Germany knows so well. And they can shift over time, as the Austrians have shown. Crucially, too, identities based on these various elements can overlap and are not exclusive. Communities can define themselves in different ways for different purposes – most obviously in the case of geography but also culturally. In some cases this is a comfortable mix; in many cases, however, it is a source of potential or actual tension (religious or ideological affiliations have often been seen as a challenge to geographic loyalties in

Europe – as shown above all by Jewish experience down the centuries, in a different way by Marxist internationalism in the 20th century, and now increasingly in many Muslim communities in Europe too).

There is therefore nothing guaranteed about the integrity of the European Union – or of its existing member states. Will all the members of the eurozone stay the course? Will some member states disintegrate? Notoriously, Spain has centrifugal tendencies, as does Belgium. In both cases, languages are the bearers of cultural identities which are regional rather than national. Italy's national identity is fragile too – though in this case the stresses are rooted in social structures and in regional history, and not in the language (without which Italy would surely have broken apart by now). The Czechs and the Slovaks separated peacefully soon after their liberation from the Soviet yoke (it is worth noting that the proposed United States of Greater Austria of 1906 had recognised their separate identities by allocating each a separate state even then). They therefore joined the EU as separate members in 2004.

Nowhere is the risk of breakup now greater than in one of the three leading members. Britain's identity is much more fragile – and has been for much longer – than its establishment has been willing to recognise until forced to do so recently. Once again, history matters. The first breakup of the single nation state on the British Isles was at least 400 years in the making. The Normans had invaded Ireland in the twelfth century, but it was Henry VIII who first proclaimed himself King of Ireland in 1541. This began the process of settling thousands of English and Scottish Protestants, displacing and dispossessing the majority Irish Catholics, suppressing their language and culture – a process which continued over generations until the abolition of the Dublin Parliament in 1801. The tragedy of the famine in the 1840s gave impetus to a struggle for Irish home rule which increasingly dominated 19th-century British politics, and which culminated in the Easter rising of 1916, the bitter fight for independence, partition and civil war. All in all, this was Britain's most shameful colonial experience.

It is doubtful whether, even today, the British have fully confronted the implications of this debacle. The British no longer tell patronising jokes about the Irish, and they have woken up to the seriousness of the Scottish claim to an independence based on their own distinctive culture. But it is not clear that the country has properly traced the real causes of this existential threat. They lie in a fragile identity welded in the 18th and 19th centuries – an identity that purported to be monolithic (and represented by a London establishment which increasingly drew Scots down from Edinburgh), centred on itself and focussed on its empire, rather than being inextricably involved with the continent of which the British Isles are a part. That identity faces being shattered again: a vote to leave the EU would be a vote to break up the UK.

Meanwhile, the Irish have found their identity in the wider context of the new Europe. If ever there was a country whose experience proves the value of the EU as what the former German Chancellor Helmut Kohl used to call the 'house of Europe', Ireland is it. Its experience through the financial and economic crisis has been far from painless: but at a deep level it has modernised and transformed itself. Its young people are well educated, digitally connected and cosmopolitan. In

one generation it has seen extraordinarily rapid secularisa-
tion (and a dramatic collapse in the moral authority of the
Church, which was historically so dominant and brooding a
presence in public life). All in all, it has acquired a new self
esteem and confidence on the international stage.

Layers of identity and loyalty

Kohl's 'house of Europe' needs to be seen against its background – a particularly German one. For better or worse, it is striking how familiar the complexity of the European identity is to the German psyche. It has historical resonances from the long-standing and subtle balances within the Holy Roman Empire. Germany is a land where over a long history people have seen themselves as involved in layered identities: the all important *Heimat*, the region, and at the same time the German culture which was defined by their language. *Heimat* has a resonance that is hard to replicate exactly in British experience. It became a focus of identity especially when people had left their home town or village behind – first during the urbanisation which accompanied the industrial revolution, and then in the very different circumstances of expulsion from the east at the end of the Second World War. Then there are the regions, with their distinctive identities and proud histories – Bavaria, Saxony, the Hanseatic city of Hamburg, and so on. The Third Reich sought to suppress all separate identities in its levelling state; so, later, did the highly centralised GDR. But the new Germany clearly shows that the ancient strong regionalism of the German lands is still a vibrant source of identity which carries real political significance.

In the darkest days of the Second World War, one of the most interesting – and poignant – of the small resistance

groups in The Third Reich is what became known as the
Kreisau circle (named by the Gestapo after the country estate
of one of its leaders, Graf Helmuth James von Moltke).[10]
Moltke was amongst the very few Germans at the time who
regarded the fall of France in 1940 as an unambiguous evil,
not as a cause for exhilaration. Their thinking about a new
order after the demise of the Third Reich would seem out-
moded in some ways (particularly as it was conditioned by
the widespread sense that the parliamentary system of the
Weimar Republic had been part of the cause of Germany's
social and moral breakdown and of Nazism's success). But
what was striking was their commitment to and advocacy of
a united European governance within which regional entities
with cohesive cultural and historical identities could exist
together in trust and at peace. Most of the Kreisau circle were
executed in 1944: but the issues they wrestled with have an
obvious and continuing relevance in the modern Europe. The
Kreisau circle is much more than just a historical curiosity,
more than just a footnote in the story of the Third Reich.

Today's German regionalism is highly stable because of
its deep historical roots. The whole lesson of German history
over a thousand years is that its identity is tied only loosely to
its polity. Because of that history, Germany is well-prepared
for today's world in which the European identity needs to be
able to enfold and embrace various specific layers of identity
– local, national, European – without demoting or cancel-
ling any of them. The threats to the British, Spanish, Belgian
and Italian identities have varying origins and may or may
not prove fatal to the integrity of these member states. But
they certainly mean that radical regional decentralisation is

inevitable. In fact, of all the larger member states, only France and Poland have little or no centrifugal tendency. But the EU offers a context in which regional identities can find their own level, either within an existing member state, as German regionalism has done so successfully in the German Federal Republic – or independently in their own member state, as the Irish experience demonstrates.

But France and Britain both face an uncomfortable reality. The shift of the centre of gravity in Europe is now clear for all to see. France has been used to the political domination of the European project ever since the start, but is now losing this position. Meanwhile, Britain would be widely welcomed -- not just by a Germany which remains distinctly uncomfortable with leadership -- as a force for the reform and openness that everyone knows is needed. But the tragedy is that Britain has been too ambivalent about its European commitment to take on this role effectively. And the fragility of its identity means that its own separatism now constitutes an existential threat to itself.

Both countries need to come to terms with the European identity to which, in truth, there is no alternative for any of us. The geographical facts, which we all share, determine our geopolitical interests. And our identity is formed through that distinctive history we are all part of, which has made us what we are, and which has endowed us with shared values that have been painfully learnt. A Europe that is – or should be – older and wiser about itself has a lot to share with others who are on the journey of modernisation.

Eurosceptics overlook the full force even of the first of these points and are naively dismissive of the second: and all too many even of the pro-Europeans underestimate the weight of the second point. Perhaps that is why European patriotism is not much in evidence amongst Europeans in these early decades of the 21st century. We do not sufficiently value – because we do not properly understand – what we offer. This absence of a strong, primary European identity has been the source of much perplexity and worry amongst the intelligentsia of Europe. Irritatingly for many, national identities have proven remarkably robust – though some are realistic enough to recognise the inevitability of this. Some question whether a strong and primary European identity is even the right objective in an increasingly globalised world.

But Europe does have shared interests, and core values which have been hard-won through history. These shared values are part of the European proposition. Other layers of identity based on history, culture and language will continue to define national, regional and local loyalties, and are also fundamental to the self-understanding of Europeans. But these common values of the Europeans are the heritage of a tradition of thought which has been shaped by such towering figures as Galileo, Erasmus, Descartes, Locke, Hume, Kant, Hegel and Darwin – and of course many others too. Out of their different perspectives, and out of the many and painful failures and wrong turnings we Europeans have taken over the generations, has emerged something profoundly important for the world of the 21st century: a commitment to rationalism, democracy, individual rights and responsibilities, the rule of law, social compassion, and an understanding of history as dynamic, open and progressive. These are worth our loyalty: this is the basis for a European patriotism.

This European loyalty could be described as a kind of constitutional patriotism. This is a term that became associated with (though it was not originated by) the German philosopher and political commentator Jürgen Habermas.[11] For him, loyalty to the constitution and the values it embodies, as opposed to any form of emotive nationalism based on culture or history, was – for obvious reasons – the only proper patriotism for his own country in the wake of the horrors of the Third Reich. Because he was reacting to Germany's particularly problematic recent history, he underplayed the importance of deep history. Some of his argumentation therefore looks superficial: in particular, he holds out both Switzerland and America as countries whose patriotism is based on loyalty to their distinctive constitutions. But that is in both cases to ignore the layers of history which define who they are, and which give strong emotional content to their patriotism. And as time goes by, it is becoming clearer that Germany's identity is not limited to a constitutional patriotism of the kind Habermas sponsored, either. Nor is any other European regional or national identity. Indeed, no true identity ever can be unencumbered by history.

On the face of it, Habermas is nearer the mark at the European level, since those European shared values are indeed reflected in the evolving efforts of the European Union to craft a constitution which embodies them and governance structures which provide efficiently and sustainably for people to realise their potential in the open world of the 21st century.

Some have speculated that the result of all this will make the European Union look like the Holy Roman Empire redivivus. Loyalty to the Empire was never much more – at least, not since the Reformation – than a loyalty to its legal traditions and its (weak) governance structure. The parallel has limited value, however. Apart from any other limitations in such a parallel between two polities which are in truth sui generis, the suggestion clearly understates the extent to which the Union will continue to impact the political life of its individual members. The story of the Empire was one of gradual fragmentation of central authority. But this is not likely to be the fate of the Union, notwithstanding the current political focus in several member states on resisting further extension of the powers of the Brussels institutions.

What the Union will indeed have in common with the Holy Roman Empire is that Union members will continue to have separate objectives and their own relationships and influence internationally. Individual member states will continue actively to market themselves – at least as commercial counterparts for the fast growing emerging economies of the world – often drawing on older connections as they do so (as in the case of Spain in Latin America). To borrow marketing terminology, there is no sign whatever of the European Union brand replacing or outshining these individual country brands.

But in the last analysis, Europe is more than just a governance structure and a set of values which we claim to reflect human worth and aspirations (and therefore, constitutional patriotism à la Habermas is not quite an adequate description of the loyalty Europe warrants). And it is certainly more than its current preoccupation with the travails of the eurozone, its loss of geopolitical influence and the ambivalence of the

British. For Europe is also the history of how we got to being a prosperous and peaceful union of peoples – a history which is both sublime and tragic, and endlessly moving. It is also a continent which is a treasure trove of beauty – for all the destruction it has seen. From its ice age art to its neolithic pottery, through classical Greece and Rome, through the Renaissance to the Romantics and down to the present day, the fruits of European spiritual, philosophical and aesthetic exploration of the human condition are, taken as a whole, the richest, most diverse, most vibrant, most searching anywhere on the planet. The overweening and overconfident imperialism has gone forever and we wince at our own pasts – this too is part of the proposition. So is the sense on the part of some that any European loyalty cannot be the last step or the highest stage of identity – that in some emergent sense we are also citizens of the world. This too is implied by those European values: this too is therefore part of Europe's painfully learned wisdom and its proposition to the world.

Where next?

So what do we do about all this? The answers differ in the different member states. For Britain, this is our most important challenge. British public opinion is more lukewarm about Europe than almost anywhere else in Europe, and Britain is the only major member state where one of the mainstream parties is deeply split over Europe. The debate about Europe in the public domain feeds on caricatures which emphasise undoubted problems with intrusive European regulation but all too rarely celebrate the benefits of the relationship. And even the pro-Europeans fail to address the real reasons why there is no alternative for Britain to a much more committed and wholehearted involvement in the European project. The good news is that the existential threat to Britain represented by a Scottish nationalism which is essentially pro-European (like its Irish counterpart) may force a more honest and realistic debate about Britain's options in the coming few years.

We therefore need: politicians who understand the realities and are prepared to speak about them; education in our schools about our European heritage and its civic implications; a media which provides a platform for serious, profound and educative debate about the European question; much greater take up by the universities of the Erasmus programme; more British civil servants taking positions in Brussels; more British parliamentary and ministerial engagement with the increasingly influential European Parliament; more British businesses involved in European dialogue, both individually and through their representative bodies and trade associations; more investment in language training at school and later in life. And much else besides. This is, in short, a challenge across the domains of British public life – political, administrative, business, educational, and for the media. To those who say that it is irrelevant to the real need – to rise to the challenge of Asia – the response can only be that they haven't understood the real nature of the Asian challenge to our identity. To rise to the European challenge is the only way to respond appropriately and sustainably to the Asian challenge.

Notes

1. Eurobarometer surveys are carried out regularly by the European Commission to monitor the evolution of public opinion in the Member States.
2. The European External Action Service was established in 2010 to bring greater coherence to the EU's foreign and security affairs policy.
3. In his 'Essay on the Principle of Population', first published in 1798, Thomas Malthus – clergyman, demographer and political economist – argued that population growth would always tend to outstrip growth in agricultural productivity. This meant that population levels would follow an inevitably cyclical pattern: living standards would decline as the population grew, leading eventually to collapse in numbers, followed by renewed growth as the cycle repeated itself. Hence, little or no sustainable growth in numbers or improvement in welfare was possible. Malthus's pessimism was an explicit reaction to the optimism of Enlightenment thinkers such as Rousseau.
4. Dean Acheson said this of Great Britain in a speech at West Point in 1962.
5. Frans Timmermans, First Vice President of the European Commission, has the cumbersomely entitled brief for 'Better Regulation, Interinstitutional Relations, the Rule

of Law and the Charter of Fundamental Rights'. His role
includes driving simplification and transparency, as well
as enforcing the principle of subsidiarity – i.e. ensuring
that Brussels does not regulate on matters which should
properly be left to member states.

6. Compare the traditional words of administration in the
   text of the first Prayer Book produced in 1549 ("The
   body of our Lord Jesus Christ which was given for
   thee, preserve thy body and soul unto everlasting life")
   with that of the more radical Protestant version of 1552
   ("Take and eat this, in remembrance that Christ died
   for thee, and feed on him in thy heart by faith with
   thanksgiving"). Now compare both with the Elizabethan
   version of 1559, which endured through all subsequent
   versions down to the Common Worship form still in
   use today. ("The body of our Lord Jesus Christ, which
   was given for thee, preserve thy body and soul into
   everlasting life: and take and eat this in remembrance
   that Christ died for thee, and feed on him in thine heart
   by faith, with thanksgiving.")

7. This treasury of wisdom surely includes such
   foundational texts for a modern understanding of
   democracy and human rights as Rousseau's *Discours
   Sur l'Origine et les Fondements de l'Inégalité parmi
   les Hommes*, published in 1754, and the *Déclaration
   des Droits de l'Homme et du Citoyen* of 1789 – not to
   mention the doctrines of August Comte (1798 –1857),
   effectively the founder of modern sociology. His themes
   of order and progress could be said to be the watchword
   of most modern policy think tank activity, and – as

evidence of their exportability – are emblazoned on the national flag of Brazil.

8. John Donne's Meditation XVII, part of his 'Devotions upon Emergent Occasions', was published in 1624. It includes the famous lines: 'No man is an island entire of itself; every man is a piece of the continent, a part of the main; if a clod be washed away by the sea, Europe is the less, as well as if a promontory were...'

9. Aurel Popovici, *Die Vereinigten Staaten von Groß–Österreich* (The United States of Greater Austria), Leipzig, 1906.

10. See Hans Mommsen, *Alternativen zu Hitler: Studien zur Geschichte des Deutschen Widerstandes* (Alternatives to Hitler: Studies in the History of the German Resistance), Munich, 2000.

11. See, for example, Jürgen Habermas, *Struggles for Recognition in the Democratic Constitutional State*, Princeton University Press, 1994.